SIMPLE HOME
IMPROVEMENTS

*your
patio &
terrace*

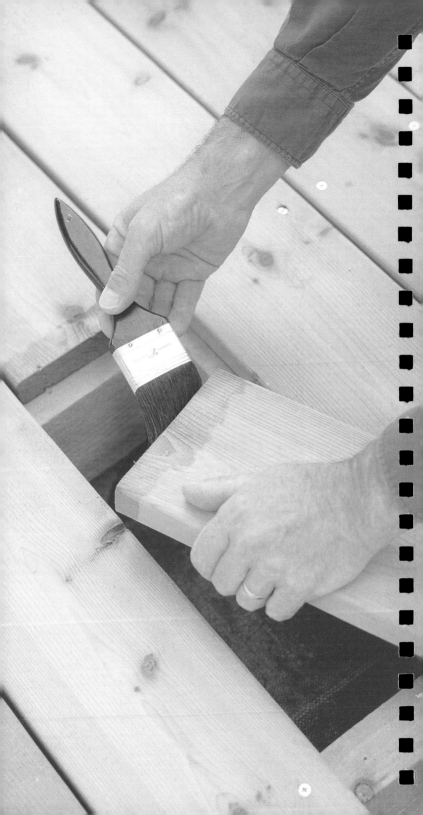

SIMPLE HOME
IMPROVEMENTS

your patio & terrace

STEWART WALTON

MARSHALL PUBLISHING • LONDON

A Marshall Edition
Conceived, edited and designed by
Marshall Editions
The Orangery
161 New Bond Street
London W1Y 9PA

First published in the UK in 2000 by Marshall Publishing Ltd

ISBN: 1-84028-386-6

Originated in Singapore by Pica.

Printed and bound in China by Excel Printing.

Project Editor Ian Kearey

Designed by Paul Griffin

Photographer Alistair Hughes

Managing Editor Antonia Cunningham

Managing Art Editor Patrick Carpenter

Editorial Director Ellen Dupont

Art Director Dave Goodman

Editorial Coordinator Ros Highstead

Production Amanda Mackie

Indexer Jill Dormon

Front cover photography: **Ron Sutherland/ The Garden Picture Library**
Back cover: **Alistair Hughes**

Note

contents

introduction

When you mention 'home improvements' to people, the great majority tend to think purely in terms of the interior and structural fabric of a building. By doing this, they are ignoring the many opportunities for creativity and improvement in a garden, whatever its size and condition. To give just one example, how often do we see a nicely tended lawn and flower borders marred by plastic chairs and tables? Away with them, and set about making stylish garden furniture from nature's own material – wood!

In this book, I designed the projects to be accessible to as wide a range of people as possible. In the introduction to each set of step-by-step photographs and text, the project is given a skill rating of Beginner, Intermediate or Advanced. Of course, to give just one example, someone with experience in woodworking, for whom cutting joints poses no problem, may find using a sewing machine a tough proposition, and the reverse will be true for a practiced tailor or seamstress.

The important thing is to look at all the stages of each project before you tackle it and, above all, take your time – the times given in the introductory section for the projects assume you have all the materials and tools to hand and can work uninterruptedly until you have finished. The additional work needed to finish a project – treating wood, applying protection, painting and varnishing – are not included in the times, nor are drying times for glue, wood filler and finishes.

For the larger-scale projects – building a patio from bricks or pavers, or building a wooden deck – I have included a rough guide to how long you can expect to take on the marking out and preparation; once this is done, the time will depend on the area to be covered and the actual materials you use.

Note that the dimensions given in the Materials lists are for the finished size of each component; you can adapt projects such as the water garden or planter to fit your own requirements. If you are planning to change the size radically, you may have to reconsider the width and depth you use for each component, both for strength and proportions.

When it comes to tools, the golden rule is that you get what you pay for. Inexpensive tools may seem a bargain, but their drawbacks can range from measuring inaccurately to falling apart while working – and for power tools, this can lead to injury or worse. Make a careful check on secondhand tools, and inspect the condition of the wiring in electrical tools.

Don't let these dire warnings put you off. If you follow the manufacturer's instructions, and wear protective clothing where necessary or prudent, you should not have a problem. Good tools do cost, so build up your tool kit as and when you can; and to save spending money on equipment that may only be used once or twice, most tool-hire stores hire out large and small power tools by the day or weekend.

I hope you get enjoyment and a sense of having achieved something worthwhile out of these projects.

Stewart Walton

chapter 1
Planters

making a water garden

This miniature water garden is ideal for a garden of any size. If your rubbish bin has handles, trim off the top of the bin just below them. You can use a wider or taller container than the one shown here, but you'll need more wood. A smaller container will need less wood.

Materials (all timber is softwood unless otherwise stated)

498-mm- (19½-in-) diameter, round, plastic rubbish bin • 1935-mm-sq (30-in-sq) plywood (for template) • 405-mm (16-in) wood strip (for template) • Screw (for template) • 16 pieces 50 x 25 x 380 mm (2 x 1 x 15 in) • 8 pieces 150 x 25 x 355 mm (6 x 1 x 14 in) • 4 pieces 50 x 25 x 100 mm (2 x 1 x 4 in) • 24 pieces 75 x 25 x 610 mm (3 x 1 x 24 in) • Brad pins • Wood glue • 38-mm (1½-in) bright zinc-plated screws • 63-mm (2½-in) bright zinc-plated screws • Exterior wood glue • Exterior wood filler • Exterior woodstain and/or varnish

Tools

Carpenter's pencil • Protractor • Combination square • Metal straightedge • Triangle with 45-degree angle • Hammer • Crosscut saw • Power drill with 3-mm (⅛-in) twist, counter-sink and screw bits • Filler knife • Coarse- and medium-grit abrasive paper • Sanding block

Skill level

Advanced

Time

8 hours

Simple home improvements

1. To make the template, drive a screw through one end of a piece of wood measuring 405 mm (16 in), and drill a hole 255 mm (10 in) away from the screw, or half the width of your container plus 13 mm (½ in), that is big enough to hold a pencil. Push a pencil through the hole so that it is flush with the bottom of the wood strip. With the screw of this tool centred on a 760-mm-sq-(30-in-sq-) sheet of plywood, draw a circle slightly larger than the diameter of your container.

2. Using a metal straightedge and triangle with a 45-degree angle, divide the circle into 16 equal sections by first making a cross to get four sections, using the triangle against the first line drawn. Divide these sections in half with a second cross, then divide the eight sections. Draw a square around the circle with the centre of each side meeting the circle.

3 Secure four pieces of 380-mm- (15-in-) long 50 x 25 mm (2 x 1 in) aligned against the outside edges of the square, using brad pins pinned down halfway. Near each end, mark where the pieces intercept the diagonal lines; mark the side edges and across the face.

4 Attach four more pieces of 380-mm- (15-in-) long 50 x 25 mm (2 x 1 in) to the work. Centre each one at a corner between two attached pieces. Make new marks on the attached pieces to note their positions, and add glue between these marks. Reposition the pieces; at each end drill two pilot holes, countersink them and drive in screws. Now remove the pins using the claw end of your hammer.

5 Use a crosscut saw or jigsaw to trim the overlapping ends flush with the adjacent pieces. At each side of the octagonal, cut the end furthest from you, then the one closer to you. Repeat steps 1–5 to make a second octagonal collar so that you have one for the top and and one for the bottom of the container.

6 On your template, mark every line that dissects the circle, measuring in 25 mm (1 in) from the circumference. Draw a line between each mark, forming an octagonal inside the circle. These marks will be used to measure the pieces that form the top, which will be used to cover the edges of the container.

7 Use the template to mark cutting lines on the eight
pieces of 355-mm- (14-in-) long 150 x 25 mm (6 x 1 in),
softwood one at a time. Align the first piece on one
side of the octagonal along the outside edge. On each
end of the work, draw diagonal lines up the side edges
and across the face. Cut along the marked lines, using
a crosscut saw or jigsaw. Work around the template
for each piece, stopping after the seventh piece.

8 To ensure a snug fit, with each cut piece in position on
the template, position the last length of wood, and use
the ends of the adjacent pieces to mark the lines on it.
After cutting the work, position it in its place on the
template, in preparation for the next step.

9 To mark the placement for the collar, lift one piece up at a time and use a combination square to transfer marks from the square on your template to the face of the pieces. Apply glue between the side edges of each piece, then repeat on the bottom surfaces of the collar that will rest on the 'top'. With the collar in position at the marks, apply glue to the top and bottom surfaces of four pieces of 100-mm- (4-in-) long 50 x 25 mm (2 x 1 in) and insert them in the gaps between the collar and top.

10 Screw down the collar, using 63-mm (2½-in) screws at the raised sections and 38-mm (1½-in) screws elsewhere. At the centre of each section, drill a pair of pilot holes, countersink them and drive in the screws.

11 Cut 24 pieces of 75 x 25 mm (3 x 1 in) to length, using the height of your container plus 6–13 mm (¼–½ in) clearance – the one shown here is 560 mm (22 in) high. For a wider container, you may need additional lengths. For a smaller container, you can use 50 x 25 mm (2 x 1 in) pieces.

12 Attach four 75 x 25 mm (3 x 1 in) pieces to opposite ends of the top and collar, aligning them flush to a corner edge of the octagon. Apply glue to one end of a 75 x 25 mm (3 x 1 in) and the surface that will be contacting the collar. With the work squared, drive in a pair of screws after drilling and countersinking the holes. Alternate between the top and bottom pieces of the collar, and make sure the screws go into the sides of the wood and not the end grain, which will cause splits.

13 Remove the work from your surface and position the bottom collar on it. After applying glue to the free ends of the 75 x 25 mm (3 x 1 in) already attached to the top collar, as in step 12, position them around the bottom collar. Follow step 12 to attach them.

14 Continue attaching the 75 x 25 mm (3 x 1 in) pieces, first to the ends of each side of the octagonal. Then attach the remaining 75 x 25 mm (3 x 1 in) pieces, centring them between the side ones.

Helpful hints

The container, with its wooden surround, can be used to pot a tree, but first drill several drainage holes in the bottom. You can fill the bottom with styrofoam peanuts to assist drainage and make the container lighter for moving.

18

15 Where the screw heads will be visible, fill in the screw holes with wood filler. Use a filler knife or old chisel to push the filler into the holes. Also apply filler to stop any gaps in the joints of the top. Allow the filler to dry completely. Using coarse-grit abrasive paper, sand down the work to remove any splinters. Also use medium-grit abrasive paper to sand the top piece – it is more likely to come into contact with people.

16 To finish your water garden, place the rubbish bin in its final position and fill in the bottom quarter with pond compost. Add a layer of gravel on top of it to keep the compost from rising to the surface of the water. For smaller plants, build a ledge with a few bricks, and place the plant on it with the top of the pot about 50 mm (2 in) below the water line.

making a **wooden planter**

A planter allows you to experiment with potted plants outside. You can choose the finish to blend in or contrast with the other features of the deck, patio or garden.

Materials (all timber is softwood unless otherwise stated)

3 pieces 100 x 25 x 1015 mm (4 x 1 x 40 in) • 2 pieces 50 x 25 x 305 mm in (2 x 1 x 12) • 4 pieces 75 x 25 x 100 mm (3 x 1 x 4 in) • 4 pieces 75 x 25 x 150 mm (3 x 1 x 6 in) • 2 pieces 75 x 25 x 1015 mm (3 x 1 x 40 in) • 2 pieces 75 x 25 x 380 mm (3 x 1 x 15 in) • 14 pieces 50 x 25 x 965 mm

(2 x 1 x 38 in) • 10 pieces 50 x 25 x 330 mm (2 x 1 x 13 in) •
4 pieces 50 x 25 x 230 mm (2 x 1 x 9 in) • 610 x 4 x 1220 mm
(24 x ⅛ x 48 in) plywood • 45-mm (1¾-in) bright zinc-plated
screws • 38-mm (1½-in) brad pins • Exterior wood glue

Tools

Combination square • Tape measure • Carpenter's pencil •
Crosscut saw • Power drill with pilot hole, screw and
13-mm (½-in) bits • Hammer • Filler knife

Skill level

Intermediate

Time

4 hours

Simple home improvements

1 For the base, clamp together three pieces of 100 x 25 mm (4 x 1 in) standing on edge. Measure and mark them at 915 mm (36 in) on the exposed edges and faces. Using a crosscut saw, cut them to length at these marks. Now clamp together two pieces of 50 x 25 mm (2 x 1 in). Measure and mark them at 255 mm (10 in), and cut them to length.

2 Set the three pieces of 100 x 25 mm (4 x 1 in) edge to edge. Position the 50 x 25 mm (2 x 1 in) pieces across the others, one at each end. Use a scrap piece of 50 x 25 mm (2 x 1 in) on edge to mark the spacing about 25 mm (1 in) in from the edges. Apply glue along one surface of the 50 x 25 mm (2 x 1 in) pieces, where they will contact the 100 x 25 mm (4 x 1 in) pieces. Centre and drive screws through each 100 x 25 mm (4 x 1 in) and fix them to the 50 x 25 mm (2 x 1 in) pieces.

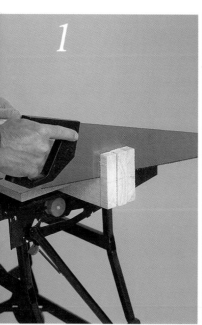

3 Drill four 13-mm (½-in) drainage holes in each 100 x 25 mm (4 x 1 in), spaced evenly apart. Place scrap wood under the work where you are drilling to prevent the work from splitting and to protect the surface.

4 Cut four pieces of 75 x 25 mm (3 x 1 in) to 75 mm (3 in) long and another four to 125 mm (5 in) long. Make a mitre cut in each one. Measure up 13 mm (½ in) from a corner, then use a combination square to draw a 45-degree angle. Clamp the wood and cut it on the waste side of the line.

Helpful hints

To save time and effort when cutting two or more pieces of timber to identical lengths, clamp them together and cut them all at once.

5 Assemble the mitred pieces to form the feet for the base. The longer ones will fit along the front and back edges; the shorter ones along the sides. For each foot, draw the position on top of the base to establish where to nail. Apply glue to all the contacting surfaces and position the pieces under the base. Then nail in brad pins about 25 mm (1 in) from each end, centred over the width of the piece.

6 For the top frame, cut two pieces of 75 x 25 mm (3 x 1 in) to 915 mm (36 in) and another two of the same dimensions to 330 mm (13 in). To mitre the ends, over-lap the adjacent pieces and square them. Draw pencil marks along the sides on each piece of wood. Draw a diagonal between the lines, and use them to cut mitres on the waste side of the lines. Mark the waste sides to ensure you mitre the corners in the correct directions.

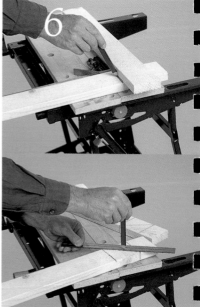

7 To make the planter box, measure, mark and cut 14 pieces of 50 x 25 mm (2 x 1 in) to 890 mm (35 in), 10 pieces to 280 mm (11 in) and 4 pieces to 190 mm (7½ in) lengths, using a crosscut saw. Again, to save time and effort, you can clamp together up to four pieces to be cut to the same length.

8 Stain the pieces, following the instructions provided by the manufacturer. You can stain them different colours if you wish – here, the top and bottom frames were stained a darker colour. Allow the stain to dry completely before you begin the assembly. You can prop the pieces on two lengths of scrap wood to prevent the stain from adhering to the work surface.

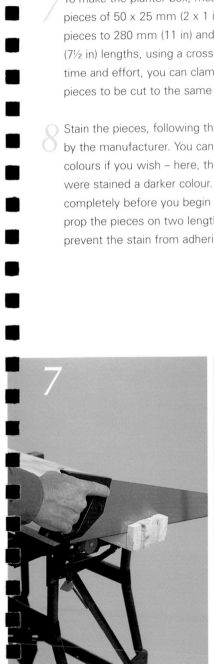

9 Cut the pieces for the bottom frame: two 50 x 25 mm (2 x 1 in) cut to 890 mm (35 in) and two cut to 190 mm (7½ in). Do a test fit to get the pieces square and centred over the base before securing them in place with screws.

10 Attach the side pieces by alternating the long and short lengths. Apply glue to each corner of the facing surfaces. Position two long pieces, making sure they are square with the ends of the bottom frame, and secure them in place with brad pins. Apply glue to each corner and secure a pair of short side pieces; alternate between the long and short pieces, saving the two 190 mm (7½ in) pieces for the top row.

11 Hold the plywood to the planter, with one edge in a corner, and mark where to cut it to length; make the cut with the saw, saving the leftover plywood for the side piece. Insert the plywood, mark the height, and cut two pieces at 785 x 293 mm (31 x 11½ in) and two at 293 x 178 mm (11½ x 7 in). Apply glue to the edges, and use brad pins to secure the plywood inside the box. Continue until all four sides are covered.

12 To secure the top frame to the box, apply glue to the contacting surfaces and secure the pieces in place with brad pins every 50 mm (2 in). If the planter will be handled often, use screws every 100 mm (4 in) – countersink the screw holes and apply filler over the screwheads (see page 19). Touch up the stain.

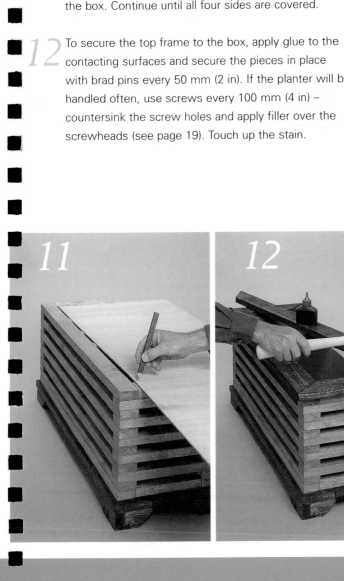

arranging a
hanging basket

Hanging baskets always look attractive above a patio or deck, and there are many designs of brackets available at garden centres and by mail order. Choose a mixture of plants, with some growing upward and others hanging or tumbling over the side of the basket.

Materials

Water-retaining granules • Soil-free potting compost • Wire basket • Bucket or large flowerpot • Coco matting or other liner • Plastic plant-pot saucer • 8 ivy plants • 2 geraniums • 6 Petunias

Tools

Trowel

Skill level

Beginner

Time

20 minutes per basket

1 Prepare the potting mixture by adding water-retaining granules to a soil-free potting mixture. Use about 50 g (1¾ oz) of granules per 5 l (1⅛ gal) of potting compost. Mix the two together thoroughly.

2 Stand the wire basket on a large flowerpot or bucket, and line the basket with coconut matting or your preferred choice of liner. Loosen the matting by pulling it apart, or 'teasing' it, as you line the basket. Place a plastic plant-pot saucer in the base of the basket, and half-fill the basket with the potting compost.

3 Plant four trailing ivy plants at this level, spaced evenly apart, pushing the roots through the matting and firming them into the potting mixture. Add more potting compost, pressing it firmly into the sides of the basket, but leaving it light and loose within the centre of the basket to allow for the rootball of the new plants. Plant a further four ivy plants to trail between the lower four.

4 Loosen the soil around the roots of the main plants, then plant the two geraniums alongside each other in the centre. Fill in all the gaps between the geraniums and the trailing ivy plants with petunias. You can use the trowel to push back the soil to make room for the new plants.

chapter 2

outdoor furniture

making a **wooden bench**

This strong, versatile bench is relatively easy to construct, and will give good service if it is weatherproofed adequately. For a rustic look, you can leave the wood slightly rough-cut, but remove any splinters or protruding slivers of wood beforehand.

Materials (all timber is softwood)

4 pieces 125 x 25 x 510 mm (5 x 1 x 20 in) • 2 pieces 100 x 25 x 255 mm (4 x 1 x 10 in) • 2 pieces 25 x 25 x 125 mm (1 x 1 x 5 in) • 2 pieces 100 x 25 x 1145 mm (4 x 1 x 45 in) • 2 pieces 150 x 25 x 1270 mm (6 x 1 x 50 in) • Brad pins • 45-mm (1¾-in) bright zinc-plated screws • Exterior wood glue • Exterior-grade wood putty • Exterior woodstain and/or varnish

Tools

Hammer • Combination square • Carpenter's pencil • Crosscut saw • Power drill with pilot hole, countersink and screw bits • Filler knife • Coarse-grit and medium-grit abrasive paper • Sanding block • Brush

Skill level

Intermediate

Time

3–4 hours

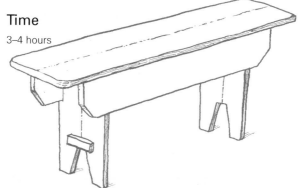

Simple home improvements

1 Place two 510 mm (20 in) lengths of 150 x 25 mm (6 x 1 in) together, making sure they are square. Nail them together with two brad pins about 100 mm (4 in) from each end. These will eventually form the legs on one end of the bench. This way, it will take less effort to cut them, and they will be exact mirrors when they are assembled.

2 Measure 418 mm (16½ in) from one end. Using a combination square, draw a line perpendicularly across the board. Rest the work on its edge and continue the line around the edge. Clamp the work in place and cut it with a crosscut saw along the waste side of the line.

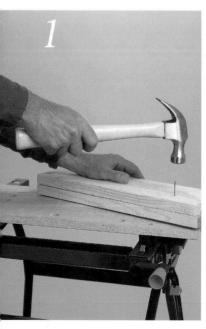

3 Measure 150 mm (6 in) from the end of the board and make a perpendicular line 38 mm (1½ in) long. At the end of the board, measure 63 mm (2½ in) in from the corner, and draw a line to the end of the first line.

4 Securely clamp the work in place on its edge, with the marks at the top. Using a crosscut saw, cut down to where the two lines meet, cutting on the waste side. Reposition the work and cut down the second line to remove the wedge.

Helpful hints

Each of the two legs is made up from two pieces of wood. These are nailed together so you can cut them to form a precise mirror image.

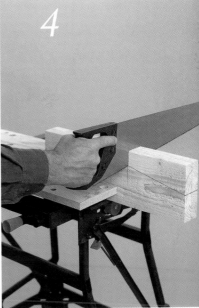

5 Hold the 100 x 25 mm (4 x 1 in) for the side of the bench on its edge along the side of the work opposite the wedge cutout. From the corner diagonal to the wedge, draw a line alongside the wood about 125 mm (5 in) long. Lie the piece down and turn it to align with the adjacent end of the work. Draw a line until it meets the first line. Use a square to square off the lines along the edges. Cut out the notch.

6 Prise apart the pieces with a chisel. Place them side by side, then lay a piece of 100 x 25 mm (4 x 1 in) along the top edges with the notch for the joint. Mark the wood at the notches and cut along the marks to about 200 mm (8 in) long. Position the 100 x 25 mm (4 x 1 in) and mark the positions for eight screw holes. Use four on each section, 25 mm (1 in) in from the edges, and four 25 mm (1 in) in from the centre. Drill pilot holes.

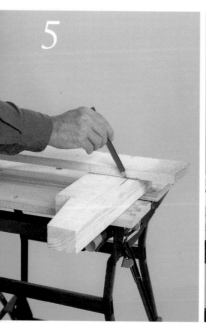

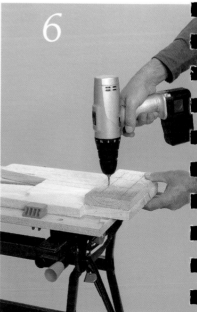

7 Countersink the holes so that the screw heads will be flush with the wood. Apply glue along the edges of the legs where they will meet, and to the surfaces that will meet between the 100 x 25 mm (4 x 1 in) support and the legs. Set the 100 x 25 mm (4 x 1 in) in place and screw the pieces together. Wipe away any excess glue with a damp cloth.

8 Cut a piece of 25 x 25 mm (1 x 1 in) to 100 mm (4 in) long to support the bottom of the legs. Drill two pilot holes about 25 mm (1 in) from the ends, and counter-sink them. Turn the legs over and apply glue to the surface above the wedge and to the 25 x 25 mm (1 x 1 in). Set the wood in position and drive the screws in; wipe away any squeezed-out glue. Repeat steps 1–8 to make the opposite legs.

9 Cut a length of 100 x 25 mm (4 x 1 in) to 1040 mm (41 in), and mitre a corner at each end. Mark the centre of the end and use the combination square to draw a 45-degree angle line to the edge. Clamp the work with the line vertical, and use the crosscut saw to cut along the line. Repeat at the opposite corner on the other end. Cut a second length in the same way.

10 Make a mark 75 mm (3 in) from each end at the top edge (without the mitres). To assemble, position one leg section with its outside edge at the 75-mm (3-in) mark. Drill and countersink a pair of pilot holes 25 mm (1 in) from the ends, centred over the main leg piece. Apply glue to the two surfaces, and drive in the screws. Continue assembling the legs and side pieces.

11 Cut two lengths of 150 x 25 mm (6 x 1 in) to 1170 mm (46 in). Mitre the corners as in step 9. Mark 140 mm (5½ in) from the unmitred end. Position the board on the bench at these marks. Centre pilot holes over the leg supports, 38 mm (1½ in) from the outside edge, and 25 mm (1 in) from the centre. Mark screw holes along the edge 268 mm (10½ in) in from these holes. Countersink the holes, apply glue to the two surfaces and along the side edge of the bench, and drive the screws in.

12 Cover the screw heads with wood filler. When it is dry, sand it flush with the surface. Sand the work to remove any splinters, starting with coarse-grit abrasive paper, then switching to medium-grit. Finish by applying a wood stain or varnish.

making a **garden table**

Designed to match the wooden bench, this timeless table uses housing joints in its construction.

Materials (all timber is softwood)

4 pieces 150 x 25 x 760 mm (6 x 1 x 30 in) • 2 pieces 50 x 25 x 305 mm (2 x 1 x 12 in) • 2 pieces 125 x 25 x 610 mm (5 x 1 x 24 in) • 2 pieces 125 x 25 x 1015 mm (5 x 1 x 40 in) • 2 pieces 100 x 25 x 610 mm (4 x 1 x 24 in) • 2 pieces 150 x 25 x 1015 mm (6 x 1 x 40 in)• 4 pieces 125 x 25 x 1270 mm (5 x 1 x 50 in) • 45-mm (1¾-in) bright zinc-plated countersink screws • 40-mm (1⅝-in) brad pins • Exterior wood filler • Exterior wood glue • Exterior wood varnish

Tools

Hammer • Combination square • Carpenter's pencil • Crosscut saw • Old screwdriver or chisel • Wood chisel • Wood or rubber mallet • Power drill with pilot hole, countersink and screwhead bits • Filler knife • Coarse-grit and medium-grit abrasive paper

Skill level

Intermediate

Time

4–5 hours

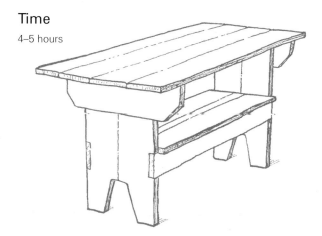

1. Nail together two 760 mm (30 in) lengths of
150 x 25 mm (6 x 1 in), using two brad pins at each
end. Set the pins about 38 mm (1½ in) from the edges
of the wood and 100 mm (4 in) from the ends. Make
sure the edges are aligned so that they are squared.

2. With a combination square, measure and mark a line
across the face of the wood about 50 mm (2 in) from
the end. Rotate the wood and continue the line along
the edge.

Helpful hints

*If you are new to woodworking, you will soon find out that
a combination square is one of the most useful measuring
and marking tools and well worth the small investment.*

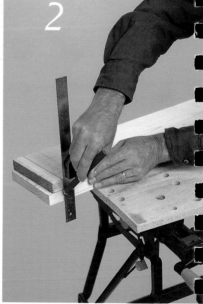

3 Cut the wood along the marked line, making sure you cut on the waste side. Measure 648 mm (25½ in) from the cut, mark another line on the opposite end and trim that end square (see page 44).

4 Decide which end is at the bottom, and then, from the bottom inside corner, measure along the length of the work 200 mm (8 in). Draw a line perpendicular to the edge 50 mm (2 in) long. From the same corner, measure 75 mm (3 in) along the short edge, then draw an angled line to the end of the 50-mm (2-in) line. Clamp the wood so the angled line is vertical for cutting, and cut along the lines on the waste side.

5 To make a notch, at the bottom outside corner measure up the length of wood 355 mm (14 in). Support the piece of 100 x 25 mm (4 x 1 in) that will be the shelf support, with its top edge at the mark, and draw guide marks on each side. Lay the work flat, then hold the edge of the 100 x 25 mm (4 x 1 in) square to the work, and use it as a guide to draw the depth of the notch.

6 Saw down the sides of the notch on the waste side of the marks (the inside of the notch); then saw cuts to the depth line every 13 mm (½ in) between the end cuts. Use a wood chisel or screwdriver to prise apart the two pieces of wood; then knock out the pins with a hammer.

7 On each piece of wood, transfer the depth mark to the other side of the work. For a neat finish, score along the depth mark, using a craft knife and metal straightedge. Clamp the work in place on top of scrap wood. Using a mallet and wood chisel, bevel the face away from the waste and remove the waste wood in the notch. Start on one side, then turn the work over and remove the remaining wood. Pare the notch to smooth it, with the chisel's bevel face down.

8 Place the two pieces of the leg alongside each other. Set a piece of 50 x 25 mm (2 x 1 in) at the top edge of the notches and mark along the notches onto the wood. Trim the wood. Mark positions for four screws 25 mm (1 in) in from each side and spaced evenly apart. Drill pilot holes for the screws, going through the top piece of wood and one-third through the second piece.

9 Use a countersink bit to make a recess for the screw heads. Apply glue to the edges of the leg pieces and between the cross support and the leg, then drive the screws in place. Wipe away any squeezed-out glue with a damp cloth. Repeat steps 1–8 to make the second 'leg'.

10 Cut two pieces of 125 x 25 mm (5 x 1 in) to 510 mm (20 in). On each piece of wood measure and mark the centre at each end. Place the blade of a combination square set at a 45-degree angle at the centre mark and draw a line along it. Use the line to make a mitre cut, using a saw.

11 Centre a table support at the top of a leg and drill two rows of pilot holes, four holes per row, spaced evenly apart and 25 mm (1 in) in from the edges. (Use scrap 50 x 25 mm (2 x 1 in) to keep the leg level.) Countersink the holes, apply glue to the surfaces of the leg and support, and drive the screws in place. Wipe away any squeezed-out glue. Repeat for the other leg and support.

12 Cut two pieces of 125 x 25 mm (5 x 1 in) to 890 mm (35 in). Assemble one length in a notch in each leg. At each end, drill a pair of pilot and countersink holes 25 mm (1 in) from the edges. Apply the glue and drive the screws in place. Wipe away any excess glue. Repeat for the second piece of 125 x 25 mm (5 x 1 in).

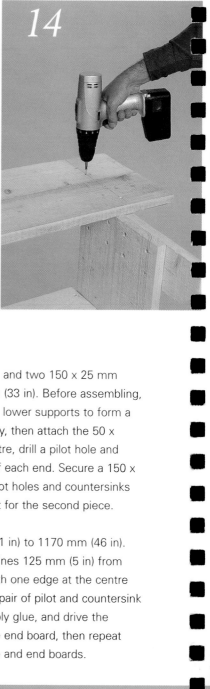

13 Cut a 50 x 25 mm (2 x 1 in) and two 150 x 25 mm (6 x 1 in) pieces to 840 mm (33 in). Before assembling, place the pieces across the lower supports to form a shelf. Trim to fit if necessary, then attach the 50 x 25 mm (2 x 1 in) in the centre, drill a pilot hole and countersink at the centre of each end. Secure a 150 x 25 mm (6 x 1 in), drilling pilot holes and countersinks and adding glue, and repeat for the second piece.

14 Cut four 125 x 25 mm (5 x 1 in) to 1170 mm (46 in). Draw perpendicular pencil lines 125 mm (5 in) from each end. Place a board with one edge at the centre of the table support. Drill a pair of pilot and countersink holes at each end, then apply glue, and drive the screws in place. Secure the end board, then repeat to secure the second inside and end boards.

Helpful hints

To save your fingers from damage when sanding – and to get the best results – make a rectangular sanding block from cork, foam or wood that will fit your hand comfortably. Fold abrasive paper over so your hand can keep it in place.

15 Cover the screw heads with exterior-grade wood filler, using a filler knife. Allow it to dry, then sand down the table, using coarse-grit then medium-grit abrasive paper to level the filler and smooth down edges that can produce splinters. Sand in the direction of the grain of the wood.

16 Apply exterior-grade wood stain and/or varnish, following the manufacturer's directions. Make sure you use the brush in the direction of the wood grain.

making a
storage box

This box will store most garden items. If you are worried
that animals may get in, attach a hasp and use a padlock.

Materials (all timber is softwood unless otherwise stated)
4 pieces 50 x 25 x 890 mm (2 x 1 x 35 in) • 4 pieces 50 x 25
x 610 mm (2 x 1 x 24 in) • 1 piece 573 x 19 x 798 mm
(22½ x ¾ x 31½ in) marine plywood • 1 piece 523 x 19 x
798 mm (20½ x ¾ x 31½ in) marine plywood • 30 pieces
460 x 88 mm (18 x 3½ in) tongue-and-groove panel • 4 pieces
50 x 38 x 610 mm (2 x 1½ x 24 in) • 1 piece 50 x 38 x 815 mm
(2 x 1½ x 32 in) • 4 pieces 75 x 38 x 610 mm (3 x 1½ x 24 in) •
3 standard 2-hole hinges with 19-mm (¾-in) screws •

2 pieces hardwood moulding 1830 mm (72 in) long • 19-mm (¾-in) veneer pins • 38-mm (1½-in) brad pins • 915-mm (36-in) chain • 19-mm (¾-in) wire staples • 4 rubber bumpers • p45-mm (1¾-in) bright zinc-plated screws • Exterior wood glue

Tools

Crosscut saw • Carpenter's pencil • Combination square • Power drill with ⅛ in (4 mm), countersink and screw bits • Hammer • Bradawl • Mitre box or tenon saw and mitre frame

Skill level

Intermediate

Time

5–6 hours

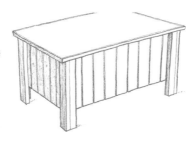

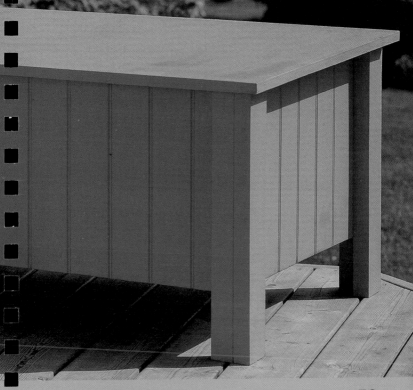

1 To make a frame, cut two lengths of 50 x 25 mm (2 x 1 in) to 798 mm (31½ in) and two lengths to 523 mm (20½ in). Join the pieces with butt joints, with the ends of the short lengths between the long ones. Rest the lengths on a flat surface, and use a combination square to mark the width of the short length on the top edge of the long one. Align the square at this mark, then place two screw marks 13 mm (½ in) from the top and bottom and centred across the width of the butting piece.

2 Drill pilot holes for the screws at your pencil mark, then countersink the holes. Apply glue to the end of the short piece, position the two pieces, using a combination square to make sure they are square, and drive in the screws.

3 Continue forming the butt joints around the frame, making sure each time that the joints are square. When drilling, make sure the opposite end of the short length is secured in place with a clamp, or set it against a sturdy object. Repeat the procedure to form the second frame. Mark the bottom surface of the frames, which should be flush, with an X.

4 Set one of the frames on a flat surface, with the marked flush surface face up, and apply glue around the top edges. Set the smaller of the pre-cut plywood pieces on top of the frame, with its edges flush with the frame. Using a length of 50 x 25 mm (2 x 1 in) set on edge as a spacing guide, draw lines parallel to the sides of the plywood with a pencil.

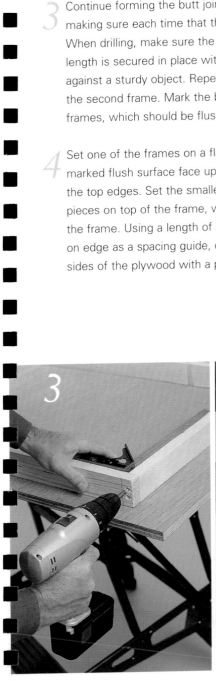

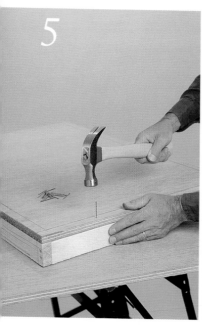

5 Centre 38-mm- (1½-in-) long brad pins between the edges of the plywood and guidelines. Hammer them in at the corners, just past the screws, then space them apart every 3 in (75 mm). Trim the tongue-and-groove panels to 15 in (380 mm) long, using a crosscut saw.

6 Set the larger pre-cut piece of plywood on the ground to create a level surface. Stand the frames on end about 380 mm (15 in) apart, with the marked flush surface of the top frame facing away from the bottom frame and the plywood end of the bottom frame facing the top frame. At each corner, attach a piece of panel to the frames (see step 7). Stagger the panels so that there is no more than one piece on each side of the box, and make sure the tongues are facing in the same direction.

7 To attach a panel, apply glue to the contacting surfaces
and nail in a pair of 25-mm- (1-in-) long brad pins at each
end. Use the combination square to keep the work
square and the panel ends flush with the frames. As
you continue to fill the side, insert the panels with the
tongues fitting into the grooves, then nail them down.

8 When you reach the end of one side, you may need to
trim a panel to fit. Use the adjacent corner panel as a
guide to mark the panel to be trimmed, then cut it
with a crosscut saw. If there is a small gap that will be
covered with a leg, you don't have to fill it.

Helpful hints

*If you have difficulty holding small nails or pins as you
hammer them in, you can poke the point of the nail through
a piece of thin cardboard, then hold the cardboard instead
of the nail as you hammer it in place.*

9 For the legs, cut four pieces of 50 x 38 mm (2 x 1½ in) and four pieces of 75 x 38 mm (3 x 1½ in) to 510 mm (20 in). Apply glue to the contacting surfaces of a length of 50 x 38 mm (2 x 1½ in) and along the corner of the front or back of the box. Drill and countersink a pilot hole 25 mm (1 in) from the top and 63 mm (2½ in) from the bottom. Drive in the screws. Attach the 75 x 38 mm (3 x 1½ in) the same way, with screws centred on the 50 x 38 mm (2 x 1½ in) at 50 mm (2 in) from the top, 75 mm (3 in) from the bottom, and one centred between.

10 To prevent fingers from being crushed by the lid, attach rubber bumpers at each corner. Centre them on the ends of the 75 x 38 mm (3 x 1½ in) sections of the legs. To support the hinges, hold a length of 50 x 38 mm (2 x 1½ in) along the back of the box along the legs. Mark their distance on the wood, then trim it with the saw.

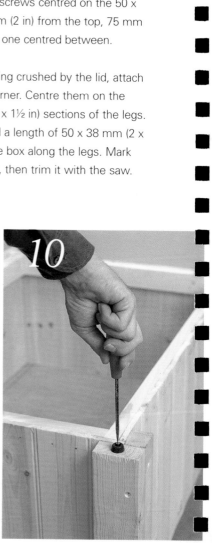

11 To install the support, apply glue to the contacting surfaces and set the wood protruding from the top edge of the box the height of the bumpers. Make pencil marks for the hinges at the centre and centred 150 mm (6 in) from the ends. Drill pilot holes, counter-sink them and drive in screws 50 mm (2 in) from either side of the centre marks for the hinges.

12 To attach a hinge, place one at its centre mark – make sure it's facing the right way up – and use a bradawl to mark the screw holes. Drill out the bradawl marks to make pilot holes, then drive in the screws.

Helpful hints

To prevent the moulding on the back edge from hitting the butt of the hinges, make hinge recesses with a chisel, or secure the moulding protruding above the lid, and plane it level.

13 Rest the box on its back and raise it off the ground to the width of the lid, using pieces of scrap wood and cardboard. Draw a centre line on the lid on the side near the box, and align this, centred on the middle hinge, with the edge of the lid aligned with the butt of the hinges. Use the bradawl to mark the screw positions on the exterior screw for the two end hinges, drill pilot holes and drive in the screws. Lift the lid up to check it is square, then insert the remaining screws.

14 With the box upright, hold hardwood moulding against the edge of one side – you can nail in a pin partway to hold it in place, but remove it after marking the wood. Draw a line up along the back side of the moulding against the lid, then angle it out away from the lid to guide you when cutting it to form a mitre. Using a mitre box or tenon saw and mitre frame, saw a mitred end.

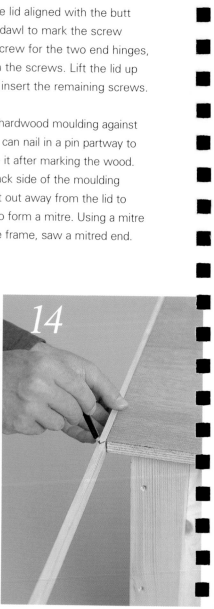

15 To secure the moulding to the lid, apply glue to the two edges, then nail in veneer pins 13 mm (½ in) from the ends and every 150 mm (6 in) apart. To measure the next piece, turn the mitred end of the unused moulding around to fit it snugly in the corner, then mark the uncut end. Make sure that you mitre the end of the second piece before measuring it. If the back strip is too wide, you may have to use a chisel to make recesses for the hinges, or set it above the hinges and plane it flush with the lid.

16 To fasten a chain to prevent the lid from flipping back, attach it with a wire staple at one end to the top frame inside the box and at the other end to the top inside corner of the lid.

making a
waterproof cushion

It's all very well making wooden benches and seats for outdoor seating, but you need cushions when sitting for a while. Instead of bringing out interior cushions and running the risk of getting them dirty or wet, you can make matching exterior ones from easily cleaned vinyl. As you become more adept at using a sewing machine and handling the fabric, you'll bring down the time needed to make each cushion.

Materials

Vinyl material • Matching durable thread • Calico • Adhesive tape • Polystyrene peanuts

Tools

Tape measure • Scissors • Sewing machine • Curved sewing needle

Skill level

Intermediate

Time

1½ hours per cushion

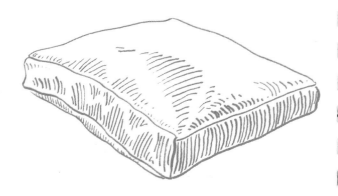

1   Measure the seat from back to front and side to side. Transfer these measurements, along with the depth that you want your cushion to be, to the back of your material, adding 16 mm (⅝ in) all around for the seam allowance. To save on material, add the pattern for the sides of the cushion to the top edges of the top, and to one side of the seat.

2   Carefully cut out the shapes along your measurement lines. Using a drinking glass as a template, draw a circle on the wrong side of the material at the centre of the seat bottom. Cut out this circle.

Helpful hints

Vinyl is a thick, stiff material to work with at the best of times, so use the largest stitch setting available on your sewing machine to stop it from splitting.

3 Cut a square of calico 50 mm (2 in) wider than the
circle. Centre it over the hole and secure it to the back
of the vinyl with adhesive tape. Stitch the two pieces
together, using the widest stitch setting on your
sewing machine. Guide the edge of the circle along
the outside edge of the pressure foot. This will be
a drainage hole if the seat gets wet.

4 With the good sides of the material facing each other,
stitch together the side pieces, leaving 16 mm (⅝ in)
of the material free at the top and bottom of the seam.
Double back at both ends of the seams to ensure they
don't pull free.

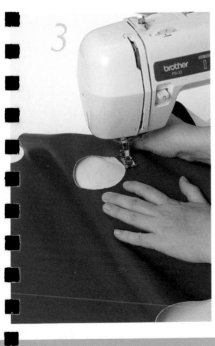

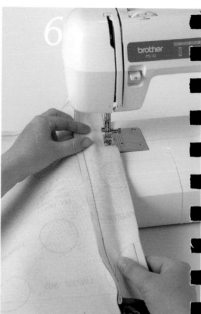

5 Attach the sides to the top with the right sides together, allowing a 16-mm (⅝-in) seam. When you reach a corner, hold the flap at the seam on the side piece flat, and stitch to the seam. With the needle completely lowered, raise the pressure foot and rotate the work. With the second flap from the side seam held flat, continue until you reach the start of this seam.

6 Sew the bottom piece to the sides with the right sides together, with a 16-mm (⅝-in) seam, allowing a 150-mm (6-in) gap. If the bottom material does not slide through the sewing machine, place a sheet of paper underneath it to help feed the material through.

7 Clip the seams at corners without cutting into the stitches. Turn the material inside out through the gap, so the right side of the fabric is exposed. Push the material out at the corners from the inside.

8 Fill the cushion with polystyrene peanuts until it is firm and flat, but without bulging. The last stage is to sew the seam at the gap, using a back stitch. A curved needle will make the stitching easier. Make each stitch about 6 mm (¼ in) long.

Helpful hints

If you have not had much sewing experience, hold the pieces of fabric together with adhesive tape or paper clips. Just remove the tape or clips before the fabric reaches the needle.

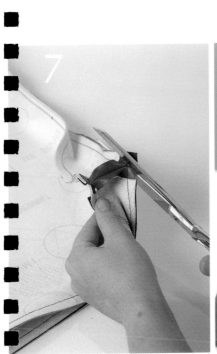

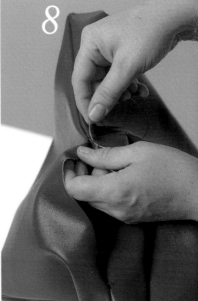

making a
plant stand

If space is limited in the garden – or even if it isn't – this
plant stand is a stylish way to display your plants.

Materials (all timber is softwood)

2 pieces 150 x 25 x 890 mm (6 x 1 x 35 in) • 2 pieces 38 x
38 x 405 mm (1½ x 1½ x 16 in) • 2 pieces 38 x 38 x 460 mm
(1½ x 1½ x 18 in) • 1 piece 38 x 38 x 760 mm (1½ x 1½ x
30 in) • 1 piece 50 x 25 x 760 mm (2 x 1 x 30 in) • 3 pieces
150 x 25 x 865 mm (6 x 1 x 34 in) • Wood glue • 45-mm
(1¾-in) bright zinc-plated screws • Wood filler • Wood stain

Tools

Carpenter's pencil • Protractor • Triangle • Crosscut saw •
Power drill with pilot, countersink and screw bits • Filler knife

Skill level

Intermediate

Time

3–4 hours

1   To mark the steps on the side piece, use a protractor
    to find a 55-degree angle and draw a line about
    100 mm (4 in) long diagonally across the board. Use a
    triangle to draw a line at a 90-degree angle from the
    first line to the edge of the board – this line should
    be 125 mm (5 in) long. From the second line, draw
    another line, 150 mm (6 in) long, at a 90-degree angle;
    then draw a fourth line at a 90-degree angle 195 mm
    (7¾ in) long. Repeat the last two measurements, then
    draw one last line at a 90-degree angle.

2   On the last line, measure down 50 mm (2 in) and draw
    a line at a 90-degree angle. From the inside angle on
    this bottom step, measure 70 mm (2¾ in) and draw a
    line at a 90-degree angle 25 mm (1 in) long. From the
    end of this line, draw another line to the point of the
    outside corner. Repeat as for the last step.

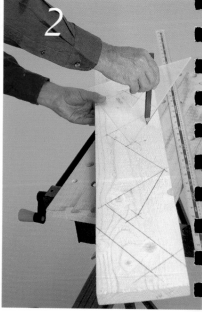

3 Clamp the work and use a crosscut saw or jigsaw to cut along the exterior lines. Use this piece as a template to mark the second side piece, and cut that.

4 To make the support pieces, measure and mark two pieces of 38 x 38 mm (1½ x 1½ in) to 355 mm (14 in) long, two to 430 mm (17 in) long, one to 660 mm (26 in) long and one 50 x 25 mm (2 x 1 in) to 660 mm (26 in) long. For the best results, make sure one end is square before measuring from it and cutting the second end.

Helpful hints

If you have a jigsaw, this is the best tool to use for cutting the angles on the side 'stepped' pieces. As with all power tools, wear protective gear and make sure you set it up properly before starting to cut.

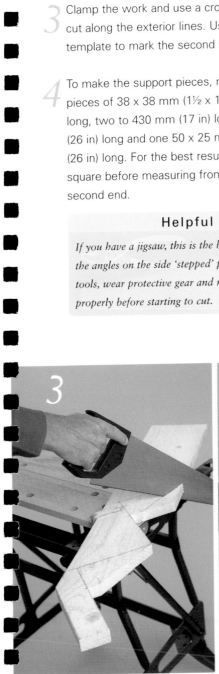

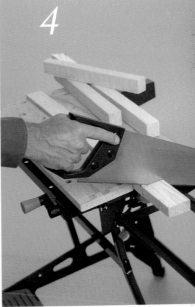

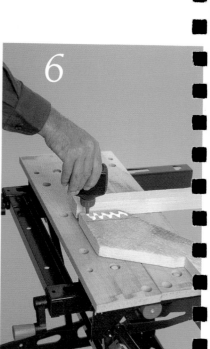

5 To assemble one side of the stand, hold a 430-mm (17-in) length of 38 x 38 mm (1½ x 1½ in) with its edge flush with the top edge of the bottom step. Hold a 355-mm (14-in) length of 38 x 38 mm (1½ x 1½ in) with its bottom edge flush with the bottom of the side piece and mark the width of the 430 mm (17 in) length on it. Mark the back side.

6 Hold the unmarked end of the 38 x 38 mm (1½ x 1½ in) length with its edges flush with the top corner of the side piece, and draw a line down its side. Apply glue in a zigzag pattern within the marked area. Screw the two pieces together (see step 8), using only one screw about 25 mm (1 in) from the end.

7 Position the 430-mm (17-in) length of 38 x 38 mm (1½ x 1½ in) with one end aligned with the marks on the 355-mm (14-in) length and the edge of the other end flush with the top edge of the bottom step. Use a combination square to make sure the two 38 x 38 mm (1½ x 1½ in) pieces are square, and mark the end and edge of the 430-mm (17-in) length of the side piece.

8 Apply glue to the marked area, and then the end of the 430-mm (17-in) length that will butt to the 355-mm (14-in) length. Screw the 430-mm (17-in) length in place, making sure the two 38 x 38 mm (1½ x 1½ in) pieces are still square. Before driving in a screw, drill a pilot hole and, if you are using a hardwood, drill a guide hole and countersink it. Add a second screw to the 355-mm (14-in) length.

9 Where the two 38 x 38 mm (1½ x 1½ in) pieces meet, drill a pilot hole centred between the two pencil marks. Countersink and drive in a screw. Assemble the second side pieces.

10 Stand the two side pieces with their front edge up. Add glue to one end of the 660-mm (26-in) length of 38 x 38 mm (1½ x 1½ in) and to the exposed end of the wood joined to the side piece. Place the 660-mm (26-in) length in position, drill a pilot hole, countersink and drive in a screw. Repeat for the other side.

Helpful hints

Accurate measuring, marking and cutting can be spoiled by screws that are inserted at the wrong angle, sometimes protruding through the wood. To avoid this, practise drilling straight, precise holes on scrap timber.

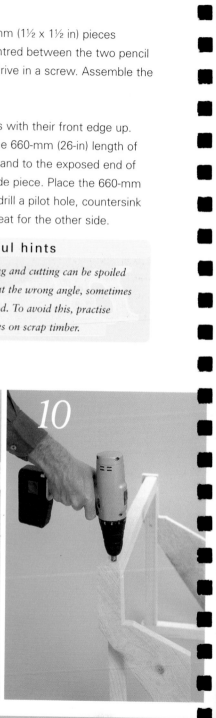

11 Apply glue to the surface of the 38 x 38 mm (1½ x 1½ in) pieces where they will meet the 50 x 25 mm (2 x 1 in). Position the 50 x 25 mm (2 x 1 in) with its ends flush to the side supports. At each end drill in a pilot hole, countersink it and drive in a screw.

12 Cut three lengths of 150 x 25 mm (6 x 1 in) to 760 mm (30 in). With the stand the right way up, install the shelves, starting at the top and working your way down. For each shelf, apply glue to the side supports, centre the shelf on the stand, and drill a pair of pilot holes centred over the side support on each end of the shelf. Countersink the pilot holes and drive in the screws. Finish off by covering the screw heads with wood filler, sanding the work down and applying a stain and/or varnish.

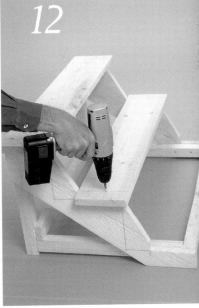

making a **brick patio**

Using bricks to make a patio or extend an existing one allows you to think creatively about the patterns you can make with the bricks. In addition, because a contrasting patio can look good, it pays to do some research into the different brick colours and textures available.

Materials

Bricks • Sharp sand • 150 x 25 mm (6 x 1 in) pressure-treated softwood • 50 x 25 x 305 mm (2 x 1 x 12 in) pressure-treated softwood wedges • 38-mm (1½-in) screws • Cement

Tools

Club hammer • Carpenter's pencil • Shovel • Spirit level • Power drill with screw bit • 3, 4, 5 triangle • Thick piece of wood • Rake • Rubber mallet • Broom • Watering can

Skill level

Advanced

Time

Minimum 8 hours

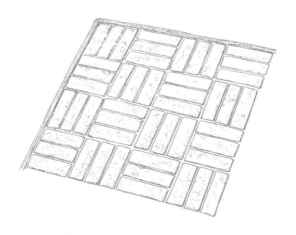

1 Lay a length of 150 x 25 mm (6 x 1 in) for one side in position, using a 3, 4, 5 triangle (see page 86) to square it to the house. Pour a line of sand along its edge, and use this as a guide to dig a trench. Set the wood in the trench snugly against the edge towards the patio and level it. Tap in a stake flush to the top of the 50 x 25 mm (2 x 1) at the end farthest from the house. Make a mark from the top equal to 3 mm (⅛ in) for every 305 mm (12 in) of patio. Tap down the 50 x 25 mm (2 x 1 in) at this end to the mark on the stake.

2 Use the triangle to square the next length of 150 x 25 mm (6 x 1 in) to the first, parallel to the house and level. Position the next length like the first, with the end farthest from the house, slightly sloping down. The last length should be level and parallel to the house.

3 To support the 150 x 25 mm (6 x 1 in) lengths, drive wedges down alongside them at the ends and every 610 mm (24 in). The top of the wedges should be about 25 mm (1 in) below the top of the 150 x 25 mm (6 x 1 in). Secure the wedges with a screw.

4 Backfill the trenches with soil, making sure it covers the top of the wedges. Tamp the soil down with a thick piece of wood.

Helpful hints

However well you lay the bricks, if the surface is not prepared accurately, the finished patio will not look good. To save on labour, consider hiring a professional to level the site for the patio.

5 Spread sand about 50 mm (2 in) deep inside the area bordered by the 150 x 25 mm (6 x 1 in). Use a rake to spread it about, then tamp it down with a piece of plywood attached perpendicular to a board, or by stamping on it. Smooth with the back of the rake.

6 Stretch a length of string parallel to the house at the end farthest from it. Work along the first pair of marks (see helpful hints, opposite) on the 150 x 25 mm (6 x 1 in). Attach each end of string to a stake, knitting needle or tent peg, and drive them into the ground to hold the string taut. Start setting out the first course of bricks. Here, we used a traditional basketweave pattern, with three bricks in one direction alternating with three bricks in the other one. Space them apart so they are set the length of a brick.

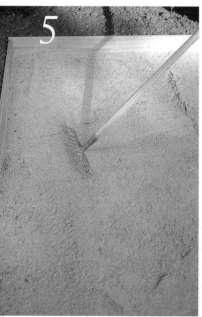

7 Move the string along for each row, and use a level to make sure the bricks are flush. If a brick is set too high, use a rubber mallet to tap it down. If a brick is set too low, push extra sand under it with a trowel.

8 Make a cement-and-sand mixture of 4 parts sand to 1 part cement. Brush it over the bricks, pushing it into the cracks. Brush away the excess and sprinkle some water into the cracks. Repeat this procedure, brushing another batch of mixture over the bricks and watering it down.

Helpful hints

To avoid cutting bricks, make the size of the patio dividable by the bricks' length. Add 50 mm (2 in) to the dimensions for the 150 x 25 mm (6 x 1 in). Draw a mark on the timber 25 mm (1 in) from the ends and each 230 mm (9 in) between.

building a **patio with pavers**

As with the brick patio, the essential starting point for this project is that the ground is level – time spent getting the early part of the procedure right will save a lot of frustration and adjusting. Before buying the pavers, look around at what is available and choose a colour and texture that will harmonize with the existing surroundings in the garden.

Materials

Concrete square pavers • Concrete edging pavers • Sharp sand • Cement • Water

Tools

3, 4, 5 triangle • Wood stakes • Club hammer • String • Spirit level • Shovel • Thick piece of timber • Rake • Broom • Watering can

Skill level

Advanced

Time

Minimum 8 hours

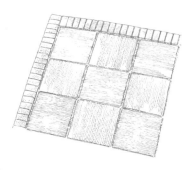

1. Start by marking where to dig a trench for the edging. Measure the area for your patio, then measure 100 mm (4 in) inside from each corner to allow the same distance of backfill soil for the edging. Place a stake inside each of these corners and drive it in, using a club hammer. Tie string to the stakes.

2. Pour a line of sand along the string to mark where you will be digging. Pour the sand directly on top of the string. Remove the string.

Helpful hints

To make a 3, 4, 5 triangle for corners, measure 915 mm (36 in) on one length of 50 x 25 mm (2 x 1), and 1220 mm (48 in) on a second length. Attach a third piece at these marks – it should measure 1525 mm (60 in) between them.

Dig a trench 100-mm (4-in) wide along the line of sand for the edging. It should be as deep as the edging pavers are long, minus 50 mm (2 in). Use the shovel to cut along the sand line. As you get to a corner, remove the stake. Fill the bottom of the trench with about 25 mm (1 in) of sharp sand.

Lay a dry run of pavers along the edges of the patio, using the 3, 4, 5 triangle at the corners to keep the rows square. Along each side, run a length of string aligned with the edges of the pavers. To establish the height of the edging bricks, drive in two stakes on each side with a club hammer, and run lengths of string 50 mm (2 in) above the top of the pavers. After the four strings are up, remove the pavers.

5 To create a slope away from the house set a length of wood on top of a stake near the house, and on the stake at the far end of the string at the other end of the house. Place a level on it and drive down the stake until they are level. For every foot of patio, lower the string 3 mm (⅛ in). For example, for a 1220-mm (48-in) wide patio, lower the string 13 mm (½ in).

6 Starting at a corner, set the edging pavers in place, standing them on end. Keep them aligned along the outside of the string, with the top edges just hitting the string.

7 Backfill the soil along the outside of the edging, then fill in the trench on the inside with sand. Use a thick length of timber to tamp down or compress the soil and sand.

8 Fill in the area of the patio between the edging with a 50-mm (2-in) layer of sand. Spread it out with a rake, then tamp it down firmly by walking over it. Finally, smooth the sand with the back of the rake.

Helpful hints

The first placement of the strings is for digging the trench for the edging, not for the pavers. To calculate pavers, subtract 100 mm (4 in) from each end of the trench.

9 Position a string line, and stakes running parallel with the line, at the end of the patio farthest away from the house. This new line should be set the width of a paving stone inside the first line. Set the first row of pavers between the sand line and the new line, using a level to keep them flush with each other and also with the top of the edging.

10 Move the string for each new row of pavers. As you continue positioning the pavers, use a rubber mallet to tap a paver that sits too high, or use a trowel to push some extra sand under a paver that is set too low. Continue until all the pavers are in place.

11 Mix a sand-and-cement mixture, using 4 parts sand to 1 part of cement. Brush this over the patio, pushing it so that it fills the cracks, then brush off any excess on the face of the pavers.

12 To help compress the mixture, sprinkle some water into the cracks. Don't, however, put in so much that the mixture splashes out. Spread the sand-and-cement mixture over the patio again, and add a little more water as required.

Helpful hints

The area covered by the pavers does not have to butt up to the house – you can position it about 610 mm (24 in) away from the house and fill the gap with gravel, pebbles, or a flower border.

building a
deck

In any yard or garden, a wooden deck makes a focal point where you can eat, relax or display a variety of plants. Before you start construction, the site where you build the deck should be cleared and level. This is hard manual labour, and you may wish to hire someone to do this while you plan the finished look.

Materials

100 x 100 mm (4 x 4 in) Southern yellow pine or pressure-treated timber, 610 mm (24 in) per post • String • Bricks or preformed concrete feet •100 x 50 mm (4 x 2 in) pressure-treated pine or other timber • 100 x 25 mm (4 x 1 in) pressure-treated timber • 460-mm (18-in) carriage bolts • Cement • Sand • Aggregate • Ground cover • Joist hangers • 38-mm (1½-in) galvanized nails • Creosote • 63-mm (2½-in) stainless-steel decking screws

Tools

Combination square • Tape measure • Carpenter's pencil • Crosscut saw • Power drill with pilot hole, countersink and 13-mm (½-in) screw bits

Skill level

Advanced

Time

Minimum 8 hours

1 Mark the area where you plan to lay your deck, using string tied around wedges driven in at the corners. Use a 3, 4, 5 square to make sure the corners are squared (see page 86). To support the deck, you'll need posts every 1220 mm (48 in) apart in rows running parallel to the house, with the rows 610 mm (24 in) apart. For each post, dig a hole 460 mm (18 in) deep, making sure the bottom is flat. Set a brick or concrete foot in the bottom.

2 Along each row of posts parallel to your house, position a length of 100 x 50 mm (4 x 2) at each side of the posts to form beams. Clamp these lengths to the corner posts about 25 mm (1 in) above the ground. Use a level vertically on the posts and horizontally on the 100 x 50 mm (4 x 2 in) to ensure they are level, then adjust and reclamp as required.

3 Drill in a pair of holes through the 100 x 50 mm (4 x 2 in) beams and posts. As you drill, pull the bit back to help remove the sawdust from the hole. Insert a pair of carriage bolts and tighten the nuts with a socket wrench. After one bolt has been inserted, you can remove one of the clamps for easier access.

4 Mix together 1 part cement to 4 parts sand and 4 parts aggregate; add a little water to just moisten it. Fill the post holes with this mixture. As you fill the hole, tamp it down with a length of 100 x 50 mm (4 x 2 in) to compress the mixture and remove any air bubbles. After the final tamping, you can finish the surface with the trowel.

5 Trim the top end of the posts flush with the top edge of the beams, using a crosscut saw with the blade at their level. Keep your free hand away from the work – the saw may jump forward as you finish the cut. If you are using pressure-treated wood, protect the cut ends from rot and insects by painting them with creosote.

6 To prevent tall weeds from growing through the deck, cover the soil with a plastic ground cover that will block out light. Lay the plastic between the rows of beams and trim it at the end with a craft knife. Cover the ends with some soil to hold it down. Don't worry if the ends do not overlap – this will allow rain water to dissipate into the ground instead of forming puddles.

7 Cut 100 x 50 mm (4 x 2 in) joists to fit between the rows of beams. To accurately mark the size, set each joist in its final position. Cut it with a saw, then nail a pair of joist hangers to each end of the beam.

8 Nail the joists to the beams, placing them centred 460 mm (18 in) apart and using 38-mm (1½-in) galvanized nails. Make sure the top edge of the joist is flush with the beams. Continue securing them between all the rows.

Helpful hints

The maximum length available for lumber is 4880 mm (16 ft). If you can keep the dimensions of the deck within this measurement, you won't have to worry about creating seams across the deck as you lay the planks.

9 With your frame now almost complete, use a straight-edge to mark the ends of the beams, then trim them with a crosscut saw. Coat all the cut surfaces with creosote as in step 5 if you are using wood that has been pressure-treated.

10 Position the first plank at the end farthest from the house and running parallel to it, protruding 25 mm (1 in) beyond the frame. Secure it with the decking screws. Drill two rows of pilot holes for the screws and space them 460 mm (18 in) apart, centred into the frame. The screws on the other planks will be screwed into the joists.

11 Lay down several planks at a time, placing 6-mm (¼-in) spacers between them. Draw a line along the front, centred over the end joist. Use this line as a guide for driving in the screws. Once all the planks are secured, trim the ends of the planks to the shortest one by drawing a pencil mark along a straightedge and cutting with a saw.

12 For a neat finish, cover the ends of the planks with a skirt, a length of 100 x 25 mm (4 x 1 in) set on end and positioned flush to the planks. Drive the screws into the end of the beams. Alternatively, you can create a shaped edge by using planks longer than your frame and trimming them. For example, in a curve or wave. If you're using pressure-treated wood, coat the cut ends with creosote, as in step 5.

chapter 4
Repairs & Improvements

repairing a **deck**

There comes a time in the lifespan of any deck when it shows signs of wear and tear, or it may suffer damage before that point. Either way, you have to do something about it, preferably before the area that needs to be replaced gets any larger.

Materials

Replacement timber • Wood preservative • Screws

Tools

Power drill with countersink and screw bits • Combination square • Carpenter's pencil • Crosscut saw • Brush • Paint bucket

Skill level

Intermediate

Time

30 minutes

1 To replace a damaged section of decking, remove the whole length of affected board by unscrewing it. With the board aligned alongside its original position, find the joists that are closest to either end of the damage. Use a combination square and pencil to draw a line along the board where it would fall at the centre of the joists – use the screw holes as a guide.

2 Use a crosscut saw to cut away the damaged wood, cutting on the waste side – the side where there is damaged wood.

Treat the cut ends of the board with a wood preservative or, if the wood has been pressure-treated, with creosote. See pages 104–112 for information on treating exterior timber.

Position the sections with the butting ends meeting in the centre of the joists. On each end, drill a pair of pilot holes, then countersink and drive in the screws through the planking and the joist.

Helpful hints

If a board has been stained or received other surface damage, as long as it has squared ends, you can simply unscrew it, turn it over and screw it back down.

treating wood for outdoor use

Even the toughest hardwood needs some degree of preservation and protection it from the ravages of the weather. The same is even more essential for softwood. Each of the methods shown here is simple: the secret of success lies in adequate preparation and meticulous working, making sure every part of the wood is treated or covered.

Materials

FOR PREPARING WOOD

Wood filler • Shellac or stopper

FOR PROTECTING PRESSURE-TREATED WOOD

Creosote

FOR PAINTING WOOD

Primer • Undercoat • Exterior-grade paint • White spirit

FOR PRESERVING WOOD

Woodstain • Wood preservative stain

Tools

FOR PREPARING WOOD

Filler knife • Medium- or coarse-grit abrasive paper
• Sanding block • Brush •

FOR TREATING PRESSURE-TREATED
WOOD

Bucket

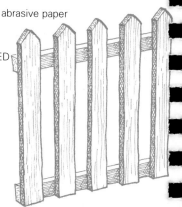

FOR PAINTING OR PRESERVING
WOOD

Brush • Paint bucket

Skill level

Beginner

Filling and splinters

You can cover screw heads, nail heads and other small holes or cracks by pressing wood filler into the recesses, using a filler knife and leaving the putty proud. Once the putty has dried, sand it smooth with abrasive paper.

To remove splinters, use abrasive paper wrapped around a cork, foam or wood sanding block. Don't worry about smoothing down rough areas. These projects are made with coarse-sawn wood to give a rustic appearance.

Sealing knots

To prevent resin from weeping out of any knots in your wood, brush shellac over them and allow to dry before the next stage. There are also proprietary knot sealers on the market – check they match the uses or woods that you intend to use.

Pressure-treated wood

If you have to cut this wood, the cut ends will need to be dipped in a bucket of creosote. Some brands of creosote are made to be brushed onto the ends. Always follow the instructions and wear protective gloves when brushing.

Natural finishes

To protect the wood while allowing its natural wood grain and colour to show through, brush on a coat of wood preservative. Always wear protective gloves and clothing if recommended.

You can add colour to your wood and still allow its grain to show through by using a wood preservative that comes ready-mixed with an added colour stain.

Paint finishes

Cover the wood with a primer, which this will prevent the paint from seeping into the wood. Brush the paint, following the grain of the wood. Allow the primer to dry, then paint on undercoat.

Next, brush on the paint. Cover any edges before painting the surfaces. Make sure you brush out any drips that accumulate in corners and under horizontal elements. You may need to apply a second coat of paint after the first one dries.

glossary

Batten – a narrow strip of wood; often used to describe such a strip used as a support for other pieces

Bevel – any angle other than a right angle at which two surfaces meet

Butt joint – a joint where two pieces of wood meet with no interlocking parts

Countersink – to cut, usually drill, a hole that allows the head of a screw, nail or pin to lie below the surface

Crosscutting – sawing wood across the grain

Galvanized – screw or nails covered with a protective layer of zinc; used mainly for exterior work

Hardwood – wood cut from trees, like oak, cherry and elm, belonging to the botanical group *Angiospermae*

Housing – a shallow, wide groove cut across the grain of a piece of wood; a housing joint is one where a piece of wood is fitted into a shallow, wide groove

MDF – medium-density fibreboard; a prefabricated material that can be worked like wood

Mitre – a joint made by cutting equal angles, usually at 45 degrees to form a right angle in two pieces of wood; cutting such a joint

Pilot hole – a small-diameter hole drilled into wood to act as a guide for the thread of a screw when driven in

Rebate – a stepped recess cut along the edge of a piece of wood as part of a joint

Ripping – sawing wood along the grain

Sanding block – a cork or plastic rectangular block around which abrasive paper is wrapped

Softwood – wood cut from trees like pine, maple and cedar, belonging to the botanical group *Gymnospermae*

Template – a cut-out pattern on paper or cardboard, used to help shape wood

index

acknowledgements

All photographs taken by Alistair Hughes, except for:

8/9 Clive Nichols/ The Nichols Gdn, Reading; 32/33 Ron Sutherland/ The Garden Picture Library; 76/77 Michael Paul/ The Garden Picture Library; 100/101 Clive Nichols/ The Nichols Gdn, Reading.

Illustrations by Stewart Walton.